Children as Peacemakers

The *Teacher-to-Teacher Series* presents personal reflections of life inside the classroom. Through the ideas presented, teachers will be inspired to exchange their own ideas with colleagues about what they do and why they do it.

Also available in the series:

On Their Way
Celebrating Second Graders as They Read and Write
Jane Fraser & Donna Skolnick

Changing the View
Student-led Parent Conferences
Terri Austin

Children Learning Through Literature
A Teacher Researcher Study
June McConaghy

Two Years
A Teacher's Memoir
Mary Kenner Glover

Children as Peacemakers

ESTHER SOKOLOV FINE

▲

ANN LACEY

▲

JOAN BAER

HEINEMANN

PORTSMOUTH, NH

Heinemann
A division of Reed Elsevier Inc.
361 Hanover Street
Portsmouth, NH 03801-3912 *Offices and agents throughout the world*

Credits begin on page 78.

Library of Congress Cataloging-in-Publication Data
Fine, Esther Sokolov.
    Children as peacemakers / Esther Sokolov Fine, Ann Lacey, and Joan Baer.
        p.   cm.—(Teacher to teacher series)
    Includes bibliographical references.
    ISBN 0-435-08851-3
    1. Peer counseling of students—Ontario—Toronto—Case studies.
    2. Conflict management—Ontario—Toronto—Case studies.
    3. Interpersonal conflict in children—Ontario—Toronto—Case studies.   4. Language experience approach in education—Ontario—Toronto—Case studies.   5. Downtown Alternative School (Toronto, Ont.)   I. Lacey, Ann.   II. Baer, Joan.   III. Title.   IV. Series.
    LB1027.5.F5   1995
    371.5'9'09713541—dc20   95-20164
                                    CIP

Cover design: Darci Mehall
Cover photo: Joan Baer
Center spread photography: Deborah Barndt
Peaceosaurus Chorus composer: Don Ross

Printed in the United States of America on acid-free paper
99   98   97   96   95   EB   1   2   3   4   5   6

This book is dedicated to Miriam DiGiuseppe (the longtime Principal of Record and much more) and to all staff past and present who helped develop the Peacemaking program at Downtown Alternative School: Mark, Linda, Judy, Petra, Lori, Christer, Debra, Marie, Genya, Jill, Andrea, Barbara, Sara, Mary Ellen, Winnie, Bernie, Bruce, and Seija; with special thanks to Carol Ledden and the staff of Brant Street Day Care, the caretaking staff, the parents, and most of all the children themselves who continue to give us hope and teach us so much about the infinite capacity of human beings to create beauty, harmony, and wisdom both in and out of school.

In Memory
Through our work on *Children as Peacemakers* we hope to carry on the ideals of our friend and mentor, Tanis Sigurjonsson, whose classroom teaching brought together a deep commitment to democracy with a respect and love for children.

Contents

Acknowledgments

The authors wish to thank the Ontario Educational Research Council, the Federation of Women Teachers' Associations of Ontario, the Toronto Board of Education, The Hilroy Foundation, the Canadian Teacher's Federation, York University, the Social Sciences and Humanities Research Council of Canada, The Educational Press Association of America, Carol Ledden and the staff of Brant Street Daycare, Deborah Barndt, Carlos Freire, Margaret McPhail, Roberta King and Ron Squire of King Squire Video, filmmaker Marjorie Beaucage, songwriter/musician Don Ross, playwright Kathleen McDonnell, *Peaceosaurus* photographer Adrian Adamson, Marie Perrier, the National Council of Teachers of English and the editors of *Primary Voices K–6*, and our editors, Carolyn Coman and Michael Ginsberg, for their generosity and support for this work on *Children as Peacemakers*.

Two Stories

The Peaceosaurus

Caitlin Burrell Daniel Nyman
Diego Filmus Nathalie Herve-Azevedo

The PEACEOSAURUS

Once upon a time there was a big, humungous, mean, dangerous, bad, fighting Dangerosaurus.

She had a baby—actually, two babies. They were both called Dangerosaurus because they were both big, humungous, mean, dangerous, bad, and fighting all the time. "You are too big and too troublesome. Go find your own home," said the big, humungous, mean, dangerous, bad, fighting mother one day, and she walked off in a big, big pout.

And the two big, humungous, mean, dangerous, bad, fighting Dangerosauruses walked off. One went one way, and the other went the other way. The oldest one fell into a swamp and died.

The other one walked off growling in a dangerous mood. It came to a big building. Children were playing ball peacefully and lovingly. It went into the playground and started bugging the children in a big, humungous, mean, dangerous, bad, fighting manner.

First, it stomped on the slide.

Then it ran through the game of kickball.

Then it stomped on someone's shoelace and broke it.

Then the kid called the Peacemakers. The Peacemakers came along and told the big, humungous, mean, dangerous, bad, fighting Dangerosaurus the Peacemaking rules:

1. Do you agree to solve the problem? Do you want to solve it with us or the teacher?
2. No running away?
3. No interruptions?
4. No name calling?
5. Tell the truth?

The big, humungous, mean, dangerous, bad, fighting Dangerosaurus said, "Maybe," to all the questions, and the kid said, "yes."

And the Peacemakers solved the problem. And now, instead of the big, humungous, mean, dangerous, bad, fighting Dangerosaurus, it is now called loveable, peaceful, nice Peaceosaurus. And now it lives in Downtown Alternative School (DAS) with its loveable, peaceful, nice, cuddly, newborn kid, and Peacemakers, and kids of many cultures and ages . . . and don't forget the teachers.

And that's how the Peaceosaurus got into DAS.

P.S. known as DASosaurus for short.

The moral of the story is: If you're mean, you won't get far, like the Dangerosaurus who drowned in the swamp.

But, if you are kind like the Peaceosaurus, you will feel happy and peaceful.

    This is our cry

    This is our prayer

    Peace on earth.

(*The PEACEOSAURUS* is a fully illustrated book, written by third graders.)

Here is another story. It is not about dinosaurs, but it carries the same message. And, it really happened.

Gina

Gina, age seven, came to Ann, her teacher, after lunch with a problem. Her face was all scrunched up, her shoulders were down, and she was twisting her long braids around her finger again and again. Gina was filled with anxiety because she had had the "same problem" with Grethel, an unresolved lunchtime problem from yesterday and the day before and maybe even the day before that. Ann gave her a choice. Either they could sit in the group to talk through the problem all together, or they could invite two Peacemakers and go off to a quiet place to work the problem through. They chose to have Peacemakers. Crystal, Grace, and Jake— a child new to the school—offered to help, and off they went. Ann listened from a distance and heard laughter break out within a couple of minutes.

Gina did not come to whine or to "tell on" Grethel. She came seeking reassurance that she and her friend were capable of working through their problem, and she came for guidance about how to begin. Whether or not these children followed a full Peacemaking ritual, they both knew that they needed to face one another and talk in order to solve their problem.

Children as Peacemakers

Introduction

This is a book about Peacemakers at an elementary school in Toronto, Canada, where children as young as three-and-a-half learn to solve their problems and resolve their conflicts without throwing sticks, stones, or words at each other. And, it is a book *of* and *about* stories. It is itself a story about one school's journey to peace—a journey taken by teachers and children—through a tangle of mistaken meanings, hurt feelings, hot tempers, and heated words.

It is through *words* and *stories* that the children and teachers at this school—Downtown Alternative School (DAS) in Toronto—find their way out of the tangle. This is *also* a story of language and of children who are learning "to language" by "languaging to learn" (Dillon, 1990) through the meanings they construct as they engage in discussion related to the social content of their school lives.

Through their work as DAS teachers, Peacemakers, and researchers, Ann, Esther, and Joan had begun to notice some important shifts. As children developed language to negotiate and resolve differences, they were beginning to *use* that language to define their experience, their interaction, and their environment. That language then became available to them in all areas of their learning. It served them when they read and when they wrote. It was there to be extended to all sorts of problem-solving tasks: social, intellectual, and material.

The DAS teachers noticed two important changes across the curriculum: The children tended to work well together in partnerships (in small groups and as a whole class), perhaps because they were learning to live with difference, resolving many conflicts as they arose. They also developed an unusual capacity to use and develop language for negotiation and collaboration, because they were discussing their environment, their relationships, and their world understandings in groups all the time. Children helped each other and shared their skills. This led to an enthusiasm for work and learning, and it seemed to produce significant changes in writing, mathematics, and artwork, while expanding the horizons of classroom research projects and scientific inquiry.

The children became clear thinkers, careful listeners, and effective language users, and they were more able to learn in an environment in which they felt safe and were confident that they would be heard and acknowledged.

The DAS story is not without its detours, wrong turns, and doubts. As is so often the case with real-life stories, this one meanders in many directions and not always reaching any final destinations. The authors of this book found that their journey to Peacemaking led them to explore issues of language development, curriculum development, negotiated curricula, and negotiations concerning power in school— how it is traditionally held and how it can be shared. The teachers, in leading children down the path toward Peacemaking, found themselves agreeing to live by some of the same rules that they were advocating for the children: respecting one another, working together, and negotiating decisions that affected them.

This book follows that meandering path. It introduces DAS before Peacemaking (Chapter 1), it retraces the steps through Peacemaking (Chapter 2), it explores the spread of Peacemaking to kindergarten (Chapter 3), it examines the complex relationship between Peacemaking and language learning (Chapter 4), it considers instances of power sharing and questions of power relationships at DAS (Chapter 5), and it reflects on the journey taken and the journey to come (Chapter 6). The story continues beyond the final pages of this book. But it can be said that the authors and the rest of the DAS community have learned that Peacemaking offers the human community a chance to avoid the dinosaur's path to extinction—if only the Dangerosauruses can become Peaceosauruses.

The Setting

1

Beginnings

Downtown Alternative School (DAS) is a small public elementary school located near the waterfront in Toronto, Canada. The school was organized by parents through negotiation with the Toronto Board of Education in 1980. It is one of many alternative public schools in Toronto that provide a different kind of schooling to a small group of children on a first-come, first-served basis. Through team teaching and a consistent program across the grades, DAS offers a whole language approach with emphasis on writing as a process. Within multiage groupings, there is room for children's intentions and their play, with respect for their intellectual capacity and ability to solve problems. Parent commitment and involvement are encouraged, and curriculum is openly discussed and negotiated with the children.

Ann, Joan, and Esther—the authors of this book—first met in 1975 at Kensington, a relatively new community public school in downtown Toronto. Joan had been teaching since 1958 and had been at Kensington since its beginning. Ann and Esther had recently graduated from a teachers' college, and Kensington was their first placement. They began as kindergarten teachers in open-area, multiage primary classrooms. Joan was a mentor and a model for them during their first years of teaching.

After a time, Joan, Ann, and Esther moved on to different schools. By the mid-1980s, Ann felt almost ready to leave teaching. She called it "classic burnout." She had been teaching a kindergarten/grade one class in a downtown area plagued by problems too numerous and severe for a school community to solve on its own. Children came to class hungry and tired. Many were depressed. Their artwork was full of bleak images, their dramatic play intense and quarrelsome. They threw pencils and erased their work so hard it rubbed holes in the paper. They resisted most efforts at math and language programming.

Ann was beginning to understand that there were many problems to solve before any school learning could take place. She began to work on the problems she thought she could tackle in the classroom: plenty of eating and food activities, lots of opportunities for play of all kinds, lots of group building. However, when two children reported instances of sexual abuse to her, and she had to deal with that process, she felt she could handle no more. She was discouraged and badly in need of a situation in which she could once again find herself as a teacher and feel some satisfaction in her work. She was feeling isolated and longed to work closely with other teachers again, as she had as a young, new teacher in 1975 at Kensington Community School.

Ann moved to Downtown Alternative School the following fall. At the time, DAS was a tiny school with only thirty-eight children at the kindergarten and early primary level. The school was rebuilding its community after a decline in enrollment. She was hired with one other teacher, Mark Cruikshank, to bring a strong child-centered, play-based program to the school.

Ann and Mark were excited about teaching together and threw themselves into their work. They had a happy and rewarding first year. Ann was relieved to find herself once again looking forward to coming to work in the morning. The dialogue, the shared observations and planning, the flexibility all energized her, and she began to feel that teaching really was the right profession for her.

Like Ann and Esther, Joan began her teaching career in a kindergarten. From the outset, she avoided workbooks and worksheets. With a strong belief in the value of play, she developed theory and practice that allowed learning possibilities to emerge within the classroom and become extended over time. Her daily plans were made at the end of each day, based on her observations and the interests of the children.

In 1984, Joan received a sabbatical leave from the Toronto Board of Education and embarked on courses for a master of education degree at the Ontario Institute for Studies in Education in Toronto. She completed her initial courses in New Hampshire with Donald Graves, Mary Ellen Giacobbe, and Nancie Atwell, whose work reinforced her belief in the inherent ability of children to solve problems and collaborate with each other. Encouraged by Ann, Joan came to teach at Downtown

Alternative School. It was 1985, her twenty-fourth year with the Toronto Board of Education.

In the spring of 1987, Esther was nearing the end of a year away from classroom teaching. She had planned to write her doctoral dissertation before September, and she was just beginning to discover how deep and challenging the writing of a dissertation can become. She saw that one year was not going to be enough, yet she was obligated to return to teaching the following September. When Ann invited her to job-share in the DAS kindergarten the following year, she accepted with enthusiasm. They would share the salary and the hours in the kindergarten, with Esther spending only ten hours of classroom teaching per week so she could continue her graduate work and complete her dissertation.

In those days, DAS was still a small primary school in the downtown garment district of Toronto, located in an old building erected in 1926 with high ceilings, wooden floors, and windows that had to be opened and closed with a long stick. In winter, more often than not, the snow blew through cracks of unsealed windows, and in June and September, they would stick shut from the humidity. DAS shared the building with Alpha Alternative School, and the two schools shared an on-site day care center (Brant Street Day Care). The DAS office doubled as a day care office in the back portion of the kitchen. Storage space was minimal. There was no staff room. Lacking the usual amenities, the caretaking staff hid out in the basement boiler room.

Planting Seeds

Joan remembers her arrival at DAS, standing in an empty classroom: no furniture, no materials, no books. But, within a short time, she was working with a multiage grouping of twenty children, ages six through eight, in an exciting environment. The DAS curriculum encompassed a solid writing process program (thanks to Joan and her mentors in New Hampshire), an individualized reading program that included "partnered" or "buddy reading," and a "borrow-a-book" (Hart-Hewin and Wells, 1988) homework program. There was an author's chair, where children read their own writing with questions and comments from the entire group. Each morning, blank paper was posted in the classroom for children to record agenda topics for discussion during class meetings.

During the same time, Joan and twelve teachers from other Toronto Board schools were involved in developing a math and science investigation program with Sister Valerie Van Cauwenberge (a mentor who was engaged in a doctoral study on the professional development of teachers). The program emphasizes hands-on materials for children to build with as they wish. In such a program, the teacher's job is to observe the children's use of the materials and support the mathematical and scientific language that evolves. Mathematical concepts from the regular math program are reinforced by the use of the building materials, a process that involves problem solving and collaboration (Toronto Board of Education, 1989).

DAS children were regularly engaging in art and science activities, while music and drama were flourishing, and one half-day per week was set aside for "building." By this time, Joan, Ann, and Esther were learning how to work as a team, and because this was an alternative school, there was a great deal of parent involvement in everyday classroom life. Many areas of the curriculum evolved in collaboration with children and parents.

For Joan, Ann, and Esther, it seemed the educational philosophy, community support, and staff at DAS had come together to create a wonderfully rich environment for teaching and learning. DAS seemed almost an ideal place for children and teachers. Almost.

The Road to Peacemaking

2

Asking Questions, Looking for Answers

Believing that they were working in the best of all possible educational worlds, these teachers were in a position to stand back, for a moment in time, to assess and examine the next step. They became concerned about children's feelings and body parts that got hurt in the yard and during the lunch period, and even sometimes in the classrooms. They became concerned about the ways in which they were dealing with these problems. They did not have a principal at the site, so they did not have the option of sending children to the office to sit until someone found time to deal with their problems. Teachers were judge and jury in all disputes, an onerous and tiresome task that siphoned their energy from the more positive and satisfying aspects of teaching.

While talking together on the playground, teachers and parents began to comment on patterns they saw in the children's play. Many conflicts repeated themselves day after day, with little serious violence but, also, with no real progress toward reconciliation. The school program, based on democratic principles and classroom practices, seemed democratic. Yet, there were still children who were fighting, hitting, ridiculing, and bullying one another on the playground and elsewhere, while teachers were still using the same old authoritarian strategies to stop, separate, quiet, and discipline them.

The teachers were not satisfied with their approach to conflict and aggression among the children. Their school was not the "warm and comfortable community of learners" (Fine, Lacey, and Baer, 1993) that they wanted.

Finding a Path

Teachers and parents continued to discuss the problem. They conducted some research, and one morning in November, a family in Joan's grade two–three class brought in a videotape about the Conflict Managers' Program that was being explored by the Community Board of San Francisco in several large inner-city schools. The class viewed the videotape, *Conflict Managers in Action* (Sadalla, Holmberg, and Halligan, 1990), and in the discussion that followed, the children—the older ones especially—were enthusiastic about becoming conflict managers. They were adamant, however, about changing the name from the more military sounding "Conflict Managers" to the gentler, more idealistic "Peacemakers."

How to start? To Joan it seemed overwhelming, but since she was used to developing curricula with children, they plunged in. They started by writing down the rules they could remember from the video and displaying them in a prominent place in the classroom.

The rules were:

1. Do you agree to solve the problem?
2. Do you want to solve it with us or the teacher?
3. No running away?
4. No interruptions?
5. No name calling?
6. Tell the truth?

Two of the eight-year-olds, Daniel and Caitlin, volunteered to be the first Peacemakers, and Joan made armbands for their identification. The armbands were worn once and were then discarded. Not needed, they ended up as scraps on the art table. Daniel and Caitlin would try to solve problems among other children in the yard and at lunchtime, and when it didn't work, the class would gather in a circle and go through the process again with those involved.

These sessions helped Daniel and Caitlin "Peacemake" particular problems; at the same time, they were modeling the process for all of the children in the classroom and for Joan, their teacher. Joan recalls having more difficulty remembering the rules than did the children. When Daniel and Caitlin became more experienced, they offered to train two more children by including them as observers in the dispute-settling process, and when they became comfortable, there were four Peacemakers in the school. Peacemaking continued in this snowballing manner. Soon there were eight Peacemakers, and then more. By the end of the school year in June, only four or five children in the classroom

had chosen not to be identified as Peacemakers. All of the children knew they could call a Peacemaker if they were having a problem. That Peacemaker, in turn, chose a second Peacemaker. When emotions were running so high that there was no time for a participant in the conflict to ask for help, anyone observing an incident could call on a Peacemaker to intervene and offer help.

When the children in conflict agreed to solve their problem and follow the rules, the Peacemakers engaged them in a formal Peacemaking exercise in which each participant had a chance to tell her or his story and be heard. The Peacemakers created a comfortable setting and encouraged the children in conflict to find agreement themselves. Peacemakers did not solve problems; rather, they helped children talk and listen to each other. Once the stories were told, suggestions for solutions were requested until one was found that all could accept. Everyone shook hands, and the Peacemakers asked if everyone was OK. Over the years, the ritual of group handshaking has remained a very important symbol for the children. It seems to signal resolution and reaffirm relationships.

The DAS teachers were not abdicating their responsibilities. The safety of the children was always paramount. Teachers remained watchful, looking after scrapes and abrasions and sometimes finding they had to separate children who were physically hurting each other. The teachers had to become models, and they, too, could call in Peacemakers to work with them to resolve a dispute. Joan recalls that choosing a child to work with her helped to "steady her up," since she had a long history as a teacher who played the roles of judge and jury.

The Peacemaking process was not a simple response to the challenge of conflict resolution. If anything, each settlement took much longer than the judge-and-jury approach, and in the process participants uncovered new layers and complexities embedded in their conflicts. The Peacemakers themselves needed to become good listeners, and they identified poor listening on the part of the children in altercations as a major hindrance to solving problems. Hence, a new rule was added: *Do you agree to listen with no arguing back and forth?*

When communication broke down at this point, an adult was called to assist, and the entire process was started again. *"Do you want to try to solve the problem? Do you want to try to solve it with a teacher or with Peacemakers?"* Given the choice, the parties usually agreed to hand the process back to the Peacemakers, with an adult hovering somewhere nearby.

The I-Message

As Peacemaking developed at DAS, another element was added: *the I-message* (Sadalla et al., 1990; Buchowski-Monin). An I-message allows the speaker to state clearly her or his experience, without judgment or blame. In explaining the concept to children, and when practicing reframing remarks and reactions in role-playing, teachers at DAS introduce the following conversation pattern:

I feel . . .
When you . . .
Because . . .
And I need . . .

Teachers at DAS found that the format could feel awkward and stilted at first, but it became more comfortable with practice. It provided a framework for children to help contain their anger while collecting thoughts. Then they could respond with care, not just react.

The teachers found that *I feel . . . and I need . . .* was a particularly good way to start Peacemaking with young children. They found that the youngest children could begin to learn to be Peacemakers from the very first day of school. These children needed good modeling of positive social skills from the adults in the room, plenty of opportunities to try out problem solving in play situations, acknowledgment for their efforts at Peacemaking, and language building (feelings and negotiation).

Teachers found they could support this process by:

• showcasing problem solving in group meeting time and asking children to bring unresolved (or partially resolved) problems to the group for input and help toward finding a solution
• practicing problem solving as a group, beginning in nonemotional situations (e.g., What rules shall we have for the handling of our pets? Teachers affirm themselves and the children as they solve problems together. Teacher: "We did a great job solving that one! The block structures aren't being knocked over anymore, now that we build in the corner.")
• giving increased responsibility to the children, with these suggestions:

1. Tell your hand to stop hitting;
2. Face the person you're having the problem with;
3. Listen, and be patient;
4. Find your own voice. Speak from the heart about your own experience. (Ask yourself: How do I feel? What do I need?);

5. Find solutions together. Make a decision to try one. (Teachers may have to give verbal support and help children to brainstorm.)

Teachers found they could gauge the emotional maturity and skill levels of the children in conflict. How much support do they need? How much can they do on their own? The children needed opportunities to conduct their own meetings, to listen and talk and try to find a solution together without the teacher. Often all they needed was reassurance from a teacher who had confidence in their ability to reconcile. Children frequently surprised their teachers by solving problems on their own or returning to play without having reached formal solutions. Sometimes an injection of humor would change the mood suddenly, and the problem would vanish. It was important, the teachers found, to let the children lead.

Peacemaking was spreading at DAS. At lunchtime and after school, Ann, Esther, and Joan would discuss role-plays and dramatizations that had arisen in the classrooms, and they would orchestrate re-enactments of these for presentation to the entire school population in the hallway (which was the one space in this small school large enough to accommodate all of the children). Such presentations usually occurred once a week. When Peacemakers were working in the yard or in the lunchroom, there always seemed to be clusters of children observing. In some cases, the observers offered possible solutions to the problem. When the Peacemaking process broke down between children from different classrooms, the protagonists from those classrooms would reassemble in a classroom setting, and the process would begin again, with teachers' support to help solve the problem and model negotiation and mediation once again.

As Peacemaking became further entrenched at the school, the adults discovered another payoff: Rather than taking valuable time out of the regular curriculum, Peacemaking was enhancing the development of language skills, listening skills, self-confidence, and a sense of ownership in a manner that fit with the rest of the curriculum and with the democratic principles on which the program was based. Many conflicts were being resolved without teachers even knowing until children told them later. Teachers felt they were learning about Peacemaking *with* and often *from* the children.

One morning, after outdoor recess, two Peacemakers came in and declared that they had been unable to resolve a problem involving three girls because one of them didn't want to solve the problem. The class gathered in a circle, and when the question was asked, "Do you want to try to solve the problem?" Maggie again clearly stated, "No!" Joan embarked on a mini lesson on democracy. She explained how majority rule meant that Maggie had to agree to try to solve the problem. Again Maggie refused. Suddenly she and Joan were involved in an angry exchange. Joan began to yell, and Maggie began to cry. The other children were silent, wondering what was going to happen next. To her dismay, Joan realized that one problem had created another problem, and she didn't know how to escape. They all resumed the school-work at hand in a shaken and negative state. Joan recalls:

> At the end of morning meeting, which was regularly used to review the morning's activities, I stated that Maggie and I had a problem and that I would like to have two Peacemakers to help us solve our problem and would Maggie agree to that. She did. And two children volunteered. The Peacemakers stated the rules and then heard my side of the story and then Maggie's side of the story and then elicited from both of us some solutions. For me, this was a powerful and pivotal moment in my learning process. The relief was so profound that without realizing it, there were tears streaming down my face, and small clear voices were emerging from the circle asking, "Are you all right, Joan?"

Maggie must have felt OK, because after the lunch break, she and the two girls who had had the original problem in the morning informed Joan that they had solved it. So, another question was added to the Peacemakers' repertoire: *"Do you want to try to solve the problem now or later?"* Sometimes the teachers choose to use children as Peacemakers when they themselves, or student teachers, have been in conflict with a child (Baer, 1994) or a group of children. The children even tried Peacemaking at home, although they reported that it was hard to apply at home because their parents didn't know the rules.

By the next year, Joan had a new group of children, but she also had a core group that was familiar with the Peacemaking process. Together, they continued to model the process during classroom time, using real conflicts. Through this process, children seemed to bring an optimism to difficulties that often defeated the more jaded adult. It was becoming clear that Peacemaking was not just another afterthought to an already overloaded curriculum. It was a powerful tool for conflict resolution, it carried powerful lessons that reinforced the overall philosophy of the school, and it was spreading (Baer, 1994).

Peacemaking Comes to Kindergarten

3

A few months after the older DAS children began practicing Peacemaking in the school yard, teachers began to see Peacemaking surface as a theme in the dramatic play of the four- and five-year-olds. Up to this point, they had done little overtly to promote Peacemaking in the kindergarten classroom. Ann spent a lot of time helping children solve their problems with each other, but she didn't yet believe that such young children could work out these conflicts on their own.

As she watched them mimic the strategies of the older children, Ann wondered how she could better support them in becoming Peacemakers themselves. Then one day, the children themselves helped Ann understand how and what they were learning. Ann wrote in her journal that night:

> Yesterday was one of those *worst* teaching days. I came home feeling bruised and battered, drained by my futile attempts to make myself heard by the four-year-old tyrants, angry at the self-centered, young, wild boys who seem to require all my attention, etc., etc.
>
> Today I am determined not to let them rule the room. A somewhat better but ragged morning—I work flat out without even a toilet break. After lunch Roger rushes in.
>
> Ann, we have to do a Peacemaking with Rick (seven years old), Martin (nearly six), and Sam (four), and it's going to be in the hall.
>
> Do you need help? Can I be there?
>
> No.

Can I be there if I don't talk?

O . . . kay.

Well I'd like to have it in here. Can you go fetch Rick?

So we call all the children over—as they are straggling to the rug.

Sam and Eric come bursting into the room late, luminescent, and changed, dragging scarves, half unzipped, "Ann, Ann, we Peacemaked outside."

(This is getting interesting. . . .) We make a circle on the rug, a small, close, intense one. It is not round because of Howard's beautiful and so-far protected structure of small blocks. I plunge in. They seem to be waiting for form. "We seem to have a problem here, but we need to understand what happened, so let's listen to each person that was involved. Sam, would you go first?"

Sam confidently lists (in some sort of order) about ten things he had been involved in (e.g., "I hit Tommy with the ball, I put snow down _____'s jacket," etc., etc.). There is also something about a big boy (other school) jumping on him. I say, "And then what, and then what?"

Finally he stops, finished. I ask Eric if he has anything to add. "No, Sam said it all." I look at them—they *feel* different, I can tell; they are not still caught in the guilt and blame. "What happened; how did you work it out?" I ask. "We Peacemaked, we told you," Sam and Eric shout together. They are jubilant. "How did you do it?" "We had a meeting in a tire." "Who was with you?" "No one, just ourselves."

What kind of resolution did they come to, and what does this have to do with Roger? Things are moving fast— I can't quite get the picture, and yet something did resolve, I think—they seem to need to *report*. What part does Roger play? Was it done to him? Does he want to be a Peacemaker for their problem? Was he an observer of a moment of resolution I may never have the privilege to witness?

It seems chaotic to me, yet I move forward on instinct. Roger's turn, and he rambles on, listing a series of wrongs and some accusations—a garbled story at best. Rick next, "Roger said it all," he says. "Oh, and it was an Alpha (the other school) boy who jumped on Sam." A few more people speak. Bella: "Sam, I hope that never ever happens to you again. It hurts my feelings to see that happen." Nancy declares: "Sometimes I even *cry* when people get hurt."

It seems to be over, the circle breaks up, and we return to normal book time. I am totally confused. What just happened?!

Later: I am discussing the incident with Susan, a student teacher. I am facing a bulletin board of children's valiant early writing efforts: scratches and scrawls of meaning, treasures. Suddenly I understand that the Peacemaking develops just like the writing. What seems random and chaotic actually contains important information—communication to us from the children about *what they know* about Peacemaking:

- you sit together to solve it
- you listen to all the sides (stories)
- you have your turn to speak
- you *report*, you tell your feelings
- you feel different at the end, and that's how you know it's the end.

They felt effective and empowered even though it was not clear to me what they had accomplished. Something important here about the absence of guilt or blame—how is that affected? By being given the space to speak? (Lacey, 1993, 1994)

Ann was thrilled to realize that the children were already teaching themselves many of the essential skills of Peacemaking:

- using a prescribed physical setup, i.e., two people in conflict facing each other
- listening
- taking a turn to speak about your experience
- coming to an ending with the other person, feeling reconciled.

By this time, there were several helpful books in print, and Ann began to read all she could find about this new field of conflict resolution. She was pleased to see how comfortably and collaboratively the DAS community was creating an effective Peacemaking program that included the type of skill building prescribed in the books. Ann also learned a great deal by reading about other approaches to conflict resolution. It became obvious that Peacemaking could work inside *and* outside the kindergarten. It was already being learned from the modeling of the older children. Any time there was a Peacemaking outside in the yard, a handful of interested children would gather around the periphery, observing and offering helpful comments. Later these scenarios would be re-enacted inside the kindergarten in the house center or the blocks.

Ann found that talking openly and helping each other solve problems at school brought a caring and sensitive tone to the classroom. At the end of a group meeting one morning, Derrick, whose constant circling often had to be ignored, burst into loud and angry tears. His battery-operated Pinocchio book had stopped working. He was absolutely inconsolable and impossible to ignore. The pressure was on, while twenty-four other children waited for direction from Ann. She talked to them about batteries getting tired, but Derrick was still crying. Becoming frustrated and anxious, Ann shoved a book hurriedly on top of the piano, knocking over her precious china model of Ping, a duck from a favorite book, *The Story About Ping*. This is how Ann described that moment:

> I freeze—we all hear it fall and break. Derrick stops crying and rushes to me. "It's just like my book!" I am almost in tears. Everyone says, "It's not your fault! The book did it!" "Can we fix it?" I ask (Can we solve this?) "YES! There's special glue!"

In Ann's classroom, Peacemaking seemed to have become the glue that held together a class of typically sensitive, emotional, young children. One year, the children had such a deep understanding of Peacemaking that they wanted to extend the "no hurting each other" rule to include feelings as well as bodies. This gave them explicit permission to try to extend Peacemaking to the more complicated emotional conflicts that come up in all relationships, including issues such as who gets invited to parties outside of school. As Ann remembered:

> We finally decided as a group that, while as individuals we had the right to choose who we invited over to "our house" to play after school, during the time we were in school together, everyone in the class should have access to all the materials and each other. This is a class of four- and five-year-olds discussing some of the problems that we adults haven't yet solved in our own relationships!
>
> The following year there were many younger and still aggressive children in the class. I had to find my way with

them; they were nowhere near ready for the in-depth discussions we had engaged in the previous year. But they had something else to teach me. One day, there was a big fight about the animal models the children used in their block play. We separated the children, wiped tears, covered scratches with Band-Aids, and sat down to try to work it out. There was a group of about eight children gathered by now. We heard the two sides, searched for solutions, but the stubborn four-year-olds weren't budging. Suddenly Bethany (herself four) blurted, "I know, let's cut them in half!" The sheer absurdity of this idea broke the tension; we all burst out laughing, and let go a little. After that, it was easier to find a compromise.

Language Learning in a Peacemaking Community

4

Peacemaking doesn't promise a problem-free environment, but it reconceives problems as opportunities and uses them, wherever possible, to build language and skills for mediation and negotiation. Peacemaking opens up traditional silences, leading children into sophisticated forms of thinking and talking.

It should not be surprising, therefore, to find a rich environment for language learning in a Peacemaking community. That is especially true when the teachers in the community believe children should select the texts that they read and write, should read and write whole texts, should read and write for a purpose, should be invited to collaborate in their reading and writing, and should publicly celebrate their successes. This chapter is a string of stories that celebrate the power of language in a language-rich community.

Peace Festival

In the spring of 1990, the DAS community held a Peace Festival with funding from the Federation of Women Teachers' Associations of Ontario (FWTAO) and the Toronto Board of Education. Toronto artists and DAS parents—a mix that included a filmmaker, a professional writer, a composer/musician—contributed to the preparation, execution, and documentation of the festival. In preparation for the festival, artists Leida Englar and Alice Norton, from a Toronto group called Shadowland, were hired to help the community develop a pageant around the theme of Peacemaking. Working in the classrooms, they helped children design costumes and build giant puppets with "found" materials, create and produce a play about Peacemaking, make musical

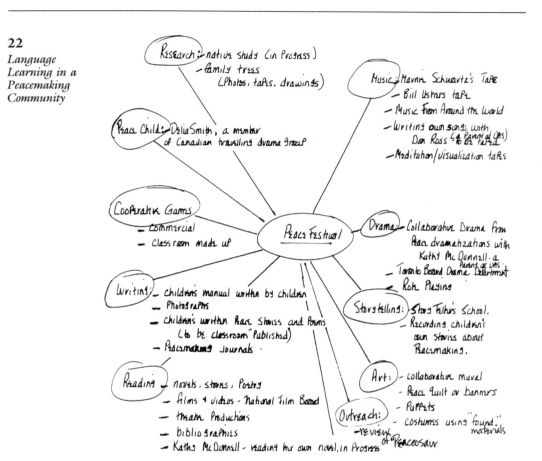

"Brainstorming" for the School's Peace Festival two months in advance: Grades 1, 2, 3

instruments for the festival parade, and set their own Peacemaking poetry to music. A short audiotape of their songs was recorded by a group of twelve DAS children—the Peaceosaurus Chorus—in a recording studio. It provided powerful background music for a six-minute video called *The Stuff That Dreams Are Made of*. The poetry comes from classroom writing by the children that year. Several of those poems and songs are reprinted below, others appear with music in the Appendix.

by Samantha

I am a Peacemaker
and I like to solve problems
with two or three people
and when you have
ten or eleven
it gets crazy and
it starts another
problem.

by Martha

Words that remind me of peace
Mother, father
on land or on sea
I like you
always near me.

by Sarah

Peace
Peace is what the world should be
Not wars or anything of that sort
If you wake up in the morning and see doves flying from
Your windows, you know it's peace
Peace is something from the section of love
If you are kind, kindness will follow you where ever you go
From the top of a mountain down to the bottom
So where ever you go, try to take peace with you
Peace is the meaning of love and friendship
So if you have peace
Don't lose it
Don't lose it.

by Julia

This weekend my Mum and Dad had a fight.
But I asked them if they wanted to peace
make and they said "Yes." So I did. The
problem was that Daddy wanted to read the
newspaper and Mommy wanted to get going.
But we solved it. I forgot what the solution was.

by Robin

Peace Fills My Heart (to music)
Peace fills my heart with love and friendship
It makes me think of a sky so blue
Peace fills my heart with love and friendship
It makes me think of a sun so bright
I wish that peace was all over the world
I wish that peace was all over
I wish that peace was all over the world.

by Daniel

(song version adapted from poem text)
Hello.
Let's talk about peace
because I like wars least.
It makes me peaceful
when I relax
not being hit
with whacks and slaps

I do not want to fight
I do not want to bite
I feel good when I'm not disturbed
So let's talk about peace
because I like wars least.

by Carla

(to music)
I wonder, I wonder
What will happen tomorrow,
Will there be peace
Or will there be war?
I wonder, I wonder
If I will be poor.
(spoken)
Peace is like a river
that goes through
Every place
In every town
In every city
In every country in the world
It goes by
Every mountain
Every house
In every village
And every valley
That is what it's like.

by Emma (to music)

Peace of the world
Peace of the world
We are the children of the world
We hold each others' hands
We are the children of the world
We hold each others' hands
And it's peace of the world
And it's peace of the world
And it's peace of the world
And it's peace of the world.

The Reading Group

Despite the high expectations of parents and teachers and the high degree of literacy in the children's homes, a few children at DAS were not yet reading in grade two. Parents of these children were becoming uneasy, and the children themselves were feeling stress as they watched their classmates start to read chapter books and engage in book-related discussions that excluded them. Adding to the stress of all concerned was the realization that the children would be facing new academic and social pressures when they transferred to neighborhood schools after completing their primary grades at DAS.

Esther puzzled over the problem. She knew that any intervention should support what the children already knew about print and books to take advantage of the cooperative learning, negotiation skills, and close, trusting friendships that the Peacemaking program had nurtured. She wanted to help the children learn to help each other make connections between print and narrative, make written text meaningful, decipher the code, enjoy and take pride in the engagements, avoid embarrassment, and have fun.

Ambitious goals, but Esther held a firm belief that her whole language approach to literacy learning held the keys. She believed that engagement with text is what matters most when readers are unlocking meanings; that reading is best developed within a supportive community in which literacy and books are valued; and that shared reading and talk about text—along with collaborative response—helps children engage in narrative as it nurtures their imaginations and supports the development of their literacy skills.

Fortunately, Esther was in a position to try to achieve her goals. As part of an expanding part-time position at DAS, she had become the resource teacher and could initiate new programs and projects. She began by borrowing an orange plastic bin from the kindergarten and issuing an invitation to this small group of children to join her at the start of the school day, three days a week, for an hour upstairs in the day care room. On the first day, they visited the small DAS library, and each child chose favorite books to place in the orange bin. Then they went upstairs and formed a circle on the carpet for discussion. They talked about books and about reading. They began by talking about how they felt about reading. They felt worried. They felt alone, but as they talked, they discovered—as good friends do—that they shared some important interests, concerns, and favorite books.

In language they could understand, Esther talked to the group about reading and reading theory. She told them about struggles she had had as a child reader and about the struggles of children she knew who eventually became excellent readers. She told them a little about child development. Some of them had learned to walk and talk at an earlier age than others, she reminded them, and all of them were now proficient at both.

With the experiences of Peacemaking to support them, Esther and the children invented the routines and rules as they needed them. They didn't need many. They were to take turns leading choral reading by sitting front and center, on the carpet, surrounded by the rest of the group, following the printed text with one finger to keep pace with the voices, which were in unison for the most part.

Esther stood at the back, out of sight. Her voice was heard, however, and it dominated at first. The children were expected to read along, but they could read silently or aloud, as long as their eyes were on the book, following the text, as the leader's finger moved across the page. Because vocalization was established as a matter of choice, silence was legitimized and the absence of voice did not signal anyone as "unable."

As a member of this reading community, Esther also chose books for the orange bin. One of her choices was *The Magic Squirrel* (Grishina, 1934), a tattered and much-loved book from Esther's own childhood with one hundred forty-one pages of dense text, large print, and black-and-white detailed drawings that were few but wonderful. The day she introduced the book, the children gasped, groaned, grew tired and achy, and required drinks in the hall. Once they started reading it together, however, they begged for extra sessions and pleaded for permission to borrow it. Esther explained that her copy was the only one in Canada. If they wanted to read it, they had to read it together with Esther present, and they had to take very good care of it. On the day they finished, the group had a party to celebrate.

By the end of grade three, these children were reading at grade level or above. They were acting as reading buddies with kindergartners and were organizing demonstrations of their reading process for their classmates. In short, they knew they were readers. In fact, as Esther reviewed a videotape made during the *second* year of the reading group, she found that most of the original members already had "graduated," and that other grade two children had taken their places.

One of the original children who remained for the second year was Tashi. He was already quite a strong reader by this time, but he liked the group, he wanted to help the others, and his confidence still needed reinforcement on a regular basis. So he elected to stay.

Only twice during the four-minute videotape do the children ask Esther for help. As with Peacemaking, she tried to provide safety and support the flow of meaning while taking as small a role as possible. And she had Tashi. He shared with the others what he had been through as a struggling reader. He gave them hope and reassurance that no adult teacher could offer. He modeled a rhythm and a sensitivity that most of the others also came to use during group reading. When some time was required to figure out a word, they learned to give that time and yet to move in before meaning was lost. The children were able to negotiate this delicate balance because they understood the reading process and were alert to each other's needs, timing, and feelings. The other children did not see Tashi as teacher, but he and Esther did; it was their special secret.

One year later Esther received a phone call from Tashi, his first contact in nearly two years. He called to reconnect and tell her how well he was doing in his new school. He wanted her to know that his teacher said he was reading two or more years above grade level. He said, "thank you."

A year later, Tashi was about to finish grade six and was an avid and strong reader. Esther showed him the videotape from the second year. She then videotaped a two-and-a-half-hour interview and discussion with him and his parents. The interview confirmed that the work on Peacemaking and reading had combined to form a successful formula for supporting a struggling reader. Tashi had developed a love of language and literature as a result of the stories he heard and read. He demonstrated that reading collaborations within a secure community extend the invitation to *all* children to become engaged readers.

The Three Little Pigs

One day in the kindergarten classroom, during a unit on recurring themes in stories from different countries, Ann was reading a version of *The Three Little Pigs* in which the first two pigs were actually eaten by the wolf. Several children were outraged. They announced, in no uncertain terms, that this was not the *real* story. Ann explained about the origins of these stories, the oral tradition, the adjustments that the storyteller must make to engage her audience, and the fact that the stories were not written down until much later. The result is different versions of the same story.

Weeks later, Ann overheard the word "version" being used in Peacemaking: "Well, that's *your* version of what happened!" Ann learned to use that word, and the fairy tales themselves, to help young children grow toward accepting the possibility of the existence of more than one version of a conflict. And the children learned how to listen better to each other.

A Story by Nina

Nina, now in grade six, has been at DAS for most of her schooling since grade one. Nina has learned about Peacemaking from other children and sees herself as a Peacemaker. She has developed a deep understanding of what it means to consider more than one possibility and entertain more than one version of a conflict.

Secret Diaries

Karl: The victim's side:
I hate Willy. I HATE Willy, and when I say HATE I mean HATE. Willy is the class bully, and I am the class wimp. So guess who Willy picks on most? Me. So here I am getting picked on by the person I hate most in the world, and what do I do? Anything he wants! Let me brief you. My name is Karl. I am ten years old, and obviously I hate Willy who is the class bully. And obviously the bully, Willy, hates me, too. So you want to know what he did to me once? We were lining up for snack, and Willy shoved me against the wall and butted me. Then when he had his snack, he took mine. I think Mr. Neckson is stupid. He never does anything. "Karl, it's time for lunch!" . . . Gotta go!
Stephanie: The observer's side:
I can't believe what Willy does to Karl. Karl is so nice. Willy is so mean. I guess it's destiny that they are enemies. I wish they weren't best enemies. I wish they were best friends, but it's never going to happen because Willy does too many bad things to ever be forgiven by Karl, even if he did want

to be friends. Why, he once put glue on Karl's chair, and Karl sat on it. Then Willy laughed. I think Mr. Neckson knows, too. I wish he would do something. "Hey Steph! Come play!" . . . Gotta go!

Mr. Neckson: The teacher's side:

That kid Willy is something else, or at least that's what the other kids say. I have never actually seen him in action. Actually, I don't think I believe them; I don't think I can! They say that Willy, "THE BULLY" got another boy, Karl, and made him eat a "chocolate covered ant." Ha! But then again . . . He might have . . . but he might not have . . . oh, well kids are smart, they can figure things out by themselves. "Mr. Neckson! I don't get this math question." . . . Gotta go.

Willy: The bully's side:

Sigh. I hate school. It's so boring. Except for one thing, . . . Karl! He is so nice! He gives me anything I want. He lets me butt in the line, he likes it when I play tricks on him, and he never gets mad. He's my best friend. No kidding! But, just a bit ago Karl said he hated me. That made me sad. I've never been that sad and tiny and helpless since Mom and Dad died in the car crash. I have lived in a foster home for two years now. I think Karl thinks I'm a bully. I'm so sad. "Willy! Time for school!" . . . Gotta go.

A couple days later:

Karl: The victim's side:

Guess what happened at school today . . . can't guess? Okay, I'll give you a detailed description: While I was in the playground, Willy came up to me (very awkwardly) and said to me, "I'm sorry, Karl, I know I was being a bully, and I'm sorry . . . will you be my friend?" "Will I?!" I said, "Sure! If you don't hit me!" So now I'm Willy's best friend, and I'm glad, even happy! (I still think Mr. Neckson is stupid, but . . . I'm happy!)

Stephanie: The observer's side:

Willy said sorry to Karl! But that's not the amazing part. The amazing part is . . . Karl said it was okay! And now they're best friends. Wow! (And Mr. Neckson didn't even do anything! Frankly, I don't think he even cares.)

Mr. Neckson: The teacher's side:

Something is strange . . . I can't quite put my finger on it.

Everybody is cooperating perfectly. It's abnormal! Everybody seems so happy and peaceful. It's terrific! I don't have to do anything, ahhhh.
Willy: The bully's side:
I am so so so so so happy! Me and Karl are best friends . . . real best friends. Forever friends. Forever ever after. Forever.

Where does this level of understanding come from in a child so young? How has Nina developed the tools to incorporate multiple voices and perspective into her writing? How does she know how to strategize her narrative so that it seems to go inside the bully experience? Nina has been an avid and sophisticated reader from an unusually early age. She knows a great deal about voice from her reading. But beyond that, Nina has for half of her life been immersed in the DAS Peacemaking program where multiple versions of reality are both expected and respected.

The Food Fight, Ta-Daa!

The Peaceosaurus was not the only book published by DAS. There is also *The Food Fight, Ta-Daa!* In 1991, Robin, a boy in grade two, wrote a script based on a continuing lunchtime problem that required repeated Peacemaking. Robin intended that his script be used in place of an improvised skit in the next DAS workshop. He auditioned his friends, and they began rehearsals on their own.

At the same time, Deborah, a DAS parent, popular educator, author, and photographer, was working with another group of children to develop a photo story that would demonstrate the Peacemaking process. The story line of Robin's script was adopted by the group, and the script was further developed by the children through discussion and improvisation. Like a DAS workshop drama, the story is based on a real problem and shows Peacemaking in action.

The original story got interrupted in the acting out, however, when a child playing a Peacemaker started stepping on the toes of another child. This unexpected turn in the drama, which was built into the photo story, only accentuates the fact that the Peacemaking process is not a recipe. It does not unfold perfectly at all times but, like everyday life, can often be a bit messy.

The final production involved graphic artist Carlos Freire, who helped edit, lay out, and design the photo story. A storyboard, sketched by Carlos before taking the pictures, was so popular with the children that it was published as a coloring book.

The Food Fight, Ta-Daa! A photo story based on a real problem . . .

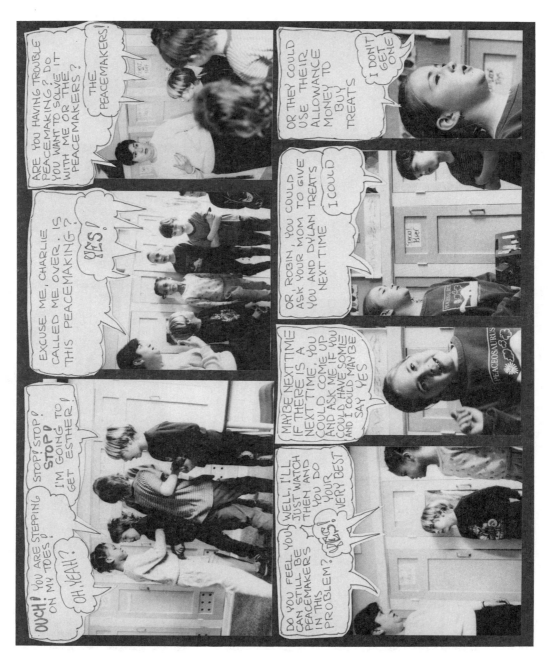

. . . and a real Peacemaking solution.

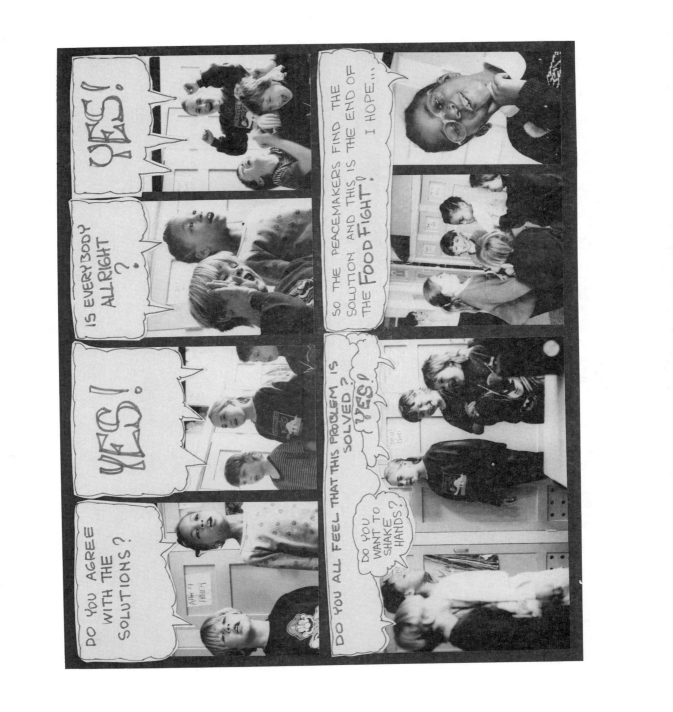

Peacemaking, Power, and Possibilities 5

Show and Tell

In the l991–92 school year, when Ann was given a sabbatical to study, write, and introduce Peacemaking to other schools, Mary Ellen came to teach in the DAS kindergarten. She began the routine of Show and Tell each morning. When Ann returned the following fall, she inherited her four-year-olds-turned-five, and they were eager to get right back into Show and Tell. She resisted mightily, and there followed what Ann later came to see as "a sort of power struggle" between herself and her class.

The kindergarten battle over Show and Tell illustrates a feature of all classrooms: the struggle for power. In every classroom, there is a subtle and shifting balance of power between teacher and children. Good teachers use their authority with care and relinquish power whenever it meets the educational and emotional needs of their children. Teachers in Peacemaking classrooms find the balance of power inevitably shifting, as the children ask for—or demand—to be heard. And, the teachers also find that when children learn to speak clearly on their own behalf and are heard, their sense of self-worth grows stronger.

This chapter highlights the transfer of power, most often without any struggles. It also raises serious questions about the nature and authenticity of mediation programs that claim to transfer power to children.

First, Show and Tell. In Ann's classroom, the children eventually won the battle. It wasn't until one of the shyest little ones, Lily asked to stand up that Ann finally understood just *what* the children had won. Lily waited patiently for the children to settle down and give her their attention, with her "surprise" held carefully behind her back, out of sight. When she was satisfied that everyone was listening, she began her presentation, pausing if there were whisperings or distractions. Lily had perfect control of the rest of the class! At the end, she asked if there were any questions or comments, and she handled these, too. Ann was stunned; she realized the children had set up their own way to practice speaking and listening, something she certainly encouraged when they were in conflict. And because Show and Tell was about the familiar little things from home, it was the perfect place to practice and develop confidence.

Parent Conferences

Power sharing doesn't always require power struggles. Sometimes power is passed simply because teachers choose to share their authority.

In this case, DAS teachers wanted the children to become more involved in communicating with parents. So, they invited the children to lead the March/April parent conferences. Children wrote their own reports, based on questions composed by the teachers. Then they prepared tasks and activities to demonstrate their learning to their parents during an interview. This required a great deal of planning, which began a month prior to the reporting date. The children wrote their reports and planned their activities during the regular school day.

With the youngest kindergartners, the children drew self-portraits for the fronts of their reports, while the teachers recorded answers to questions such as: How old are you? Do you know your telephone number? How can you tell when you are getting close to your house? Do you need help with anything at school? What do you know about Peacemaking? Parents tried to identify their child's picture. The children shared their art folders and a favorite book with their parents. Then they spent time together painting, playing a game, or using building materials.

In addition to self-portraits, the older children wrote responses to questions such as: What are your three favorite books? What are your three favorite art and math activities? They described what they thought good readers and writers have to do, what they liked about themselves, and what they knew about Peacemaking. Some described situations in which they used Peacemaking. When their parents came for the interview, the children read their reports to them, showed their writing file folders, and read one of their stories or compositions. They read something of their choice from the classroom library and demonstrated a math problem or a science experiment.

Before reporting day, parents signed up for a time to attend; and on reporting day, parent(s) and child sat together for a meeting that lasted approximately thirty minutes. There were as many as four or five conferences in different parts of the classroom simultaneously. The facilitators within family groups were the children. The teacher moved among groups—listening, assisting children, and talking with parents.

After the group conferences, there was a social get-together in a central space in the classroom with cookies and juice prepared by the children and teachers. Parents, too, often brought homemade treats to share. Like Peacemaking, these conferences demonstrate how children can take control of their own learning and communicating. If only we let them.

Children's Comments Following Child-led Parent Conferences
"*My interview* was nice because I don't always get to show my mom and dad my work, and I was kind of scared because it was my first time doing an interview. Oh, and also it was fun when I did my math activity because I had never shown it before."

"*I liked* showing my word because I am the one who really knows what I am learning."

"*It's fun* because I don't have to wait 'til my parents come home to know what the teacher said about myself."

"*I liked* my parent interview because I got to spend more time with my parents, and I got to show my parents all my work from September to March."

"*I think* my mom and dad got to know more about me."

Children's Responses to Peacemaking
On their reports children were asked to respond to the following questions about Peacemaking:

1. What do you know about Peacemaking?
2. How did you become a Peacemaker?
3. Describe a situation when you used Peacemaking.

The following are children's comments about Peacemaking extracted from dictated and written reports:

Caitlin (age five)
"It's for peace . . . we do Peacemaking when people are fighting. Kids do it. They ask questions like: What was happening before? The teacher helps."

Josh (age five)
"I know to say the rules. No hitting. No interrupting. No running away. No punching. No kicking."

Jesse (age four)
"It's for calming you down."

Shane (age four)
"That you're not supposed to hit. If I see a problem I go running there, and I solve it. And I say, 'No running away, no plugging your ears. Is everyone listening?' Then we say, 'What's your story?' Whoever's listening most I pick first. The other person comes along. We say, 'It's your turn.' And they say their problem. And we say, 'Do you want to play together or do you want to share? Or, should we get another ball?' Then it's all solved. I know a lot of things. I used to be a Peacemaker, but now I like to have fun. If there's a problem in North America, how could I go there? It's too far!"

Lina (age five)
"The big kids do it. It's for problems. They do it to get peace. They choose who goes first for talking. Then they choose a different person. It gets to be over from questions and comments."

Pippy (age five)
"No kicking. Don't plug your ears. No punching. When the Peacemaker says something you have to listen, and you tell both sides. I'm a Peace-

maker. When my brother came to be a Peacemaker I wanted to be one so I did."

Alex (age four)
"For solving problems. Well, I'm just starting to learn the rules about Peacemaking. I watch my brother. 'No running away,' and 'No plugging your ears.' Then they start Peacemaking. It's over when the problem's solved."

Marjorie (age five)
"It's for making friends again. I think you might Peacemake these kids in our class, but I don't know how."

Natalie (age four)
"Having a problem. Nina can do it, Ann. I did some of a Peacemaking. I told someone to have a turn later on the swing."
Ann: "Did it help the problem?"
Natalie: "Yes it did."

Max (age six)
"Because if somebody gets in a fight and this is not a fight school. We have Peacemaking. You talk about it. There are rules of Peacemaking. We have two Peacemakers."

Natalie (age six—two years later)
"Because the school has fighting. No running away. No saying that it isn't true. No interrupting."

Cory (age seven)
"Listen to the rules: Speak one at a time. Don't interrupt. Don't fight. Don't run away. Don't plug your ears. Wait your turn to talk."

Leah (age seven)
"Rules: No saying things that are not true. No walking away. No interrupting when other people are talking. Peacemakers ask who wants to speak first. Then the person who is picked says their part of the

story. Then the other person says their part of the story. Then they say 'Sorry' and they shake hands."

How I Became a Peacemaker by Nora (age seven)
I was six. Well, I became a Peacemaker when Bob came over and said, "Will you help me with a problem?" And I said, "All right, I'll be a Peacemaker." But it was kind of hard because I had never done a Peacemaking before, and I didn't know the rules . . . so Bob said everything. The people in the problem were Amanda and Beverly and a few other people. I didn't know what solutions were, I kept asking, "What are solutions?" I kept asking, and no one would listen to me. Finally someone told me what solutions were so I suggested a solution. My solution was that they should shake hands and say sorry to each other, and so they shook hands and said sorry to each other. And everybody clapped because it was my first Peacemaking (Fine, Lacey, Baer, Rother, 1991/92).

My First Peacemaking by Emma (age six)
I watched other people, and then I learned how to be a Peacemaker. I saw people fighting. It was a looooong time ago. I was five, and then somebody came up to me and said, "Can you be a Peacemaker?" And I chose a Peacemaker. I chose Ida, and then we started to Peacemake, and then we came to solutions. I didn't have a solution, but Ida did and then the Peacemaking was over, and that's it. I've been a Peacemaker for a long time (Fine, Lacey, Baer, 1993).

My First Peacemaking by Chloe (age five-and-three-quarters)
Well, it was building day for Joan's class, and there was a problem and John and Davie were involved, and they asked Greg to be a Peacemaker, and Greg picked a Peacemaker which was me. And a long time ago, I was looking at some people solve a problem for the workshop, and I saw them do the rules and the Peacemaking, so I knew a little bit, and I could Peacemake with Greg. That's all.

Branching Out
During the very first year of Peacemaking, the DAS community was invited to give a presentation at another school. They went as a group: teachers, several parents, and six children presented together. The teachers and parents described the school and the Peacemaking process. The

children dramatized problems and showed how they used Peacemaking to try to solve them. At the end, the entire group fielded questions. The children were astonishingly informative and articulate. They handled most of the discussion, while teachers and parents sat back in amazement and learned from them.

Since that time, the DAS community has presented many workshops, and each has been different. A large number of DAS children have had turns to present at at least one workshop. Some have presented many times. They've re-enacted problem situations and have described what was current in the Peacemaking program. As the children have learned to speak, listen, and engage in discussions to plan these workshops, they've begun to discuss effective ways to teach others what they were learning. They've asked themselves and each other what an audience might want to see and hear and how to sequence events so that their messages would be clear. As they've struggled to make these messages understandable to others, the children have refined and extended their own thinking and language.

As the DAS children have developed the language and social skills needed to solve problems, they have become increasingly skilled at working and learning in groups. They've become more caring and more aware of the needs of others. They've begun to feel safe and confident that they will be heard and acknowledged, and they've expressed pride and ownership in school—pride and ownership that they certainly have earned.

Critical Questions

In 1991, Esther was hired by the Faculty of Education at York University to teach and supervise students in the first year of a three-year undergraduate teacher education program, and in the summer of 1993 she taught her first graduate course.

Most of the York undergraduates come with a great deal of previous experience with children in classroom, day care, and other settings. Esther has explored various ways of introducing Peacemaking to her students and generally finds them receptive. She has imported the DAS workshop—children and all—to classes at York, and she has listened in awe to her university students as they talked with tiny DAS presenters, their parents, and teachers. Still greater was her awe as she listened to the tiny presenters, some with still quite limited social skills, describe the work of the Peacemakers they envision themselves becoming.

Esther has invited presenters from other host schools to introduce a range of conflict resolution models to the student teachers. She has assigned informal observations, requiring the students to watch and share information about conflict resolution programs in their host schools. She also has assigned readings and shown videotapes concerning conflict resolution and asked students to role-play a problem and then engage in Peacemaking in small groups. She is still developing this part of her course and knows she has a lot of work ahead as she tries to bring Peacemaking into teacher education in a more comprehensive way. She feels strongly that work on Peacemaking should become one of the basics of teacher education.

Esther has attempted to fold the concept of Peacemaking into her graduate course on Reading, Writing, and Critical Literacy. She sees clear links between *how* children read, write, talk, and think and *what* they read, write, talk, and think about. Esther sees Peacemaking as a logical and useful entry point to issues of gender, race, class, language, dialect, and power relations (Fine, 1987, 1989, 1990, 1991).

> We believe that Peacemaking has the potential to create comfortable and supportive social and linguistic spaces that allow children to recognize safe choices and shift positions. When we ask children in our Peacemaking programs, "Do you want to solve the problem?" we are presenting them with our own hopes and expectations for positive change. We are offering a sense of possibility. (Fine, 1994)

Along with the possibilities are the doubts. In her master's research project (1993), Franca Li Preti asks these questions about conflict resolution programs:

> To what degree are student facilitators, or conflict managers, involved in the democratic governance of the whole school? Are students empowered to take action into their own hands, or does administration have the final veto in the decision-making process? Who has the last word concerning the selection process for conflict managers: students or teachers? Are the student facilitators encouraged to change the structure of the training sessions and/or meetings if they find them to be irrelevant? Is the power

structure bottom-up or top-down? Who is empowering whom to do what?

It became clear to me [Li Preti explains], after examining one program, that there was actually little room for student empowerment. Student facilitators seemed to act like "robots" for the school's "discipline machinery," following a set of commands dispatched by the adult authorities in the school. At the training sessions and meetings, students were lectured to by teachers with facts from a pre-packaged curriculum. . . . [I]t would seem that the student facilitators were being used as subordinates who followed dictated rules and regulations set by the administration.

All school-based conflict resolution programs share important goals: to demonstrate to young people that they have many choices besides aggression or passivity for dealing with conflict and to provide them with the skills to make these choices real in their own lives. The common mission for educators is to find alternatives to violence as they help children learn to resolve and learn to live with differences. Conflict resolution programs should not become ends in themselves.

Students should not be encouraged to join or stay in the program simply because there are tangible rewards and bonuses. The students have to internalize the program's philosophy of peaceful, non-confrontational resolution. Most important, conflict managers should be trained by professionals to identify, label and help resolve conflicts that are racially or ethnically motivated. Conflict managers need to be empowered by their knowledge, skill, awareness, and sensitivity to intervene in incidents involving racial injustice and to recognize when a problem needs to be referred to the adults in the school (Li Preti, 1993, 1994).

Another voice in the discussion of the value of conflict resolution is that of Margaret, a DAS parent from the early days—the mother of Caitlin, who, along with Daniel Nyman, volunteered to be the first two Peacemakers. Margaret's younger child, Lesley, was in the DAS kindergarten at that time. The following is an excerpt from an article written in 1990 by Margaret for the DAS parent newsletter in which she explains her thoughts and feelings about Peacemaking. She starts by explaining that, as a secondary schoolteacher, she saw violence and other antisocial behaviors rewarded by attention in the schools. Peacemaking seemed worth trying as an alternative to traditional methods of handling conflict, but Margaret was skeptical. She is skeptical no longer.

> The first factor to play a role in shifting my perspective occurred when my older daughter left DAS. I began to hear stories of school life in which this or that person had been unfairly blamed for something that had occurred. Often it was a case of physical violence, in which well-intentioned teachers had stepped in to end the problem before someone got seriously hurt, and sent the perpetrator off packing to the office.

> The intended message was that violence was not to be tolerated. But behind the outward display of violence there was often another story. . . a story of racist taunts, or of a person being harassed and ignored when s/he asked the harasser to stop. These situations somehow never came to light because the focus was on the violent reaction, rather than on the more subtle violence provoking it.

> . . . As I discussed the issues with others, sat in meetings, re-assessed philosophies and programs, etc. I began to see that the strength of the Peacemaking program was not only in the fact that it encouraged listening to others and their problems. The power was also—and perhaps more important—in the fact that it gave those involved a *voice* and an avenue to exercise that voice effectively and appropriately. Moreover, there were no externally meted-out punishments or rewards giving rise to feelings of being treated unjustly— the outcomes were self-imposed limits and changes that were agreed upon after an opportunity to articulate your point of view, to explore the overall picture and to incorporate your point of view into the whole picture in a way that involved neither complete submission nor dominance.

> . . ."It's not fair!" is a phrase we often hear and a feeling we often experience. It seems to me that often it is a cry that comes from not having our story told and in that way validated, rather than from an assertion that we are not "in the wrong . . ."

Margaret ended the debate with herself by asking, "Do I believe all this stuff?" And she answered, "I'm not sure, but it leads me off in a new direction I'll have to explore." While others involved in Peacemaking might have been more emphatic in their endorsement of the process, all of them join Margaret in looking for new directions and possibilities to explore.

Changes and Transitions 6

Moving . . . and Moving On

In the fall of 1993, DAS was moved across town, after an eighteen-month process of consultation with the Toronto Board of Education. The process seared through the community; many people were determined not to leave the old site. There were endless meetings, and an outside facilitator was eventually hired to help community members find common ground, so that they could move forward with some sense of unity. In this context, it was difficult for the adults to use the Peacemaking skills they had taught the children. They had to continually remind themselves that they were good at solving problems. Finally, the move happened at the end of school, and the year went out on a weary note.

Those who did move with the school were looking forward to the new building, with lots of storage space, room to spread out, and room to expand to grade six over the next three years. But they could not have predicted what impact the move would have. The changes are too numerous to list, but they involved space and staff changes, and half the community was new. It was hard to keep the strong sense of identity they had once had. The staff was not unified; there were many new children, and they were now situated within a residential community that already had a strong sense of its own identity.

What happended to Peacemaking in all this? With so many of the older Peacemakers gone and so many adults who were new to Peacemaking, who was going to model it? Ann's questions pressed on her mind, "Should we (could we?) start at the beginning again? And exactly where would that be?" As the teacher who had been there the longest, and the one assigned Peacemaking as one-half of her job in the new school, she felt a strong responsibility to maintain the high profile of Peacemaking. But there were other pressing problems to solve, and she knew Peacemaking couldn't be forced on anyone. There had to be a genuine willingness on both sides to solve problems. (*Do you agree to solve the problem?*) She also knew that people have to feel safe before they can reveal their feelings in conflict. And change does not encourage feelings of safety.

So the teachers began to do a little of everything they knew: a mini refresher course. The older children enjoyed performing role plays in small groups, but they were not settled enough in their own class to try it out on their own problems. Experienced adults continued to try to model the Peacemaking structure. Ann found few children who wanted to use the rules, though they did earnestly want to listen better and speak out clearly for themselves. With the middle group of children (grades two and three), Ann was able to generate lots of games and activities that supported the skills some of these children had practiced in kindergarten. These helped their understanding of Peacemaking to grow deeper.

In addition to particular Peacemaking skills, it seemed necessary to do lots of connecting and community building among the children. This included shared outside and inside playtime, lunchtime visits, buddy reading, whole school trips to a familiar play or to the country, sharing art projects, talent shows, and more. Some of these activities were initiated by adults and many by the children themselves.

By its second year, the "new DAS" was beginning to settle into its new skin. The rhythms of the seasons in the building and neighborhood had become familiar the second time around, and maybe everyone was a bit less anxious. The DAS story, like all school stories, was about starting and then starting over again.

What We Have Learned, Lingering Questions, Visions

In the fall of 1991, Ann was invited to conduct a pilot project for the Toronto Board of Education, implementing conflict resolution programs in eleven schools across the city—schools that varied tremendously from neighborhood to neighborhood. Most were junior kindergarten to grade six schools; a few were junior kindergarten to grade eight schools. Some were "inner-city" schools, some were in wealthier neighborhoods, and a few had a French immersion stream. Ann found she had to start in a different place in each school. Most of the children she worked with were willing to start trying out role plays.

young children develop understanding and respect for other people's stories, their needs, and their points of view.

The ultimate questions are these: If adults nurture and respect children's relationships with each other, will the children take more responsibility for relationships and value them more? In other words, does Peacemaking teach children how to value relationships and build connections with each other? Is that what it is all really about in the end? So, the teachers and children of Downtown Alternative School continue to gather on the carpet and ask, "Do you want to solve this problem?"

Endnote

In April 1993, Esther was awarded a major research grant by the Social Sciences and Humanities Research Council of Canada. This three-year ethnographic study involves extensive videotaping within DAS classrooms and in the school yard to observe language development and linguistic negotiations in the DAS community.

Appendix

For Joan, Ann, and Esther, writing this book has been a rich experience of meaning-making and peaceful problem-solving at kitchen tables and greasy spoons all over Toronto. It is a celebration of collaborative possibility. Along the way, we have found that sometimes the work of children moves into profound moments of art, poetry, prose, and music. A few examples follow.

Peace Fills My Heart   Robin

Peace fills my heart with love and friendship
It makes me think of a sky so blue
Peace fills my heart with love and friendship
It makes me think of a sun so bright
I wish that peace was all over the world
I wish that peace was all over
I wish that peace was all over the world

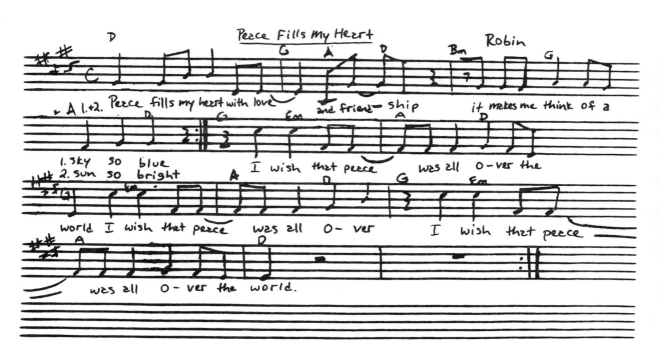

Let's Talk About Peace   Daniel

Let's talk about peace, 'cause I like wars least (2)
I feel peaceful when I can relax
Not being hit with whacks and slaps
Let's talk about peace, 'cause I like wars least

Let's talk about peace, 'cause I like wars least (2)
I don't wanna fight
I don't wanna bite
Let's talk about peace, 'cause I like wars least

Peace of the World   Emma

Peace of the World (2x)

We are the children of the world } 2x
We hold each others hands

And it's
Peace of the World (4x)

PaECE oF THE WoRLD
THE CHiLdRen oF THE
WORLD We HOLD Each oTHeR's
hand's and iT's PaECE oF
THE WORLD

BY Emma

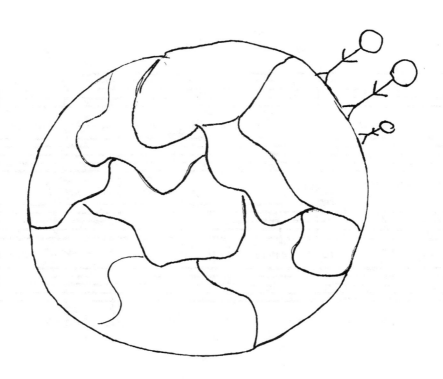

I Wonder

by Carla

I wonder, I wonder what will happen tomorrow?
Will there be peace, or will there be war?
I wonder, I wonder what will happen tomorrow?
Will we be rich, or will we be poor?

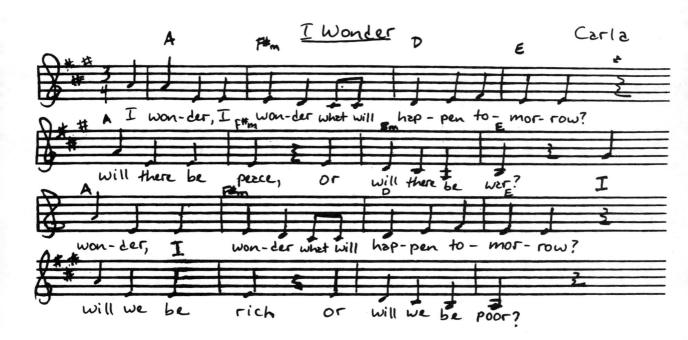

① ♡ Peace. ♥

Peace and love fills
our heart with happiness.
Peace is nice, but war
is dark and ugly. I don't
like war, and I am sure
that all of us don't
like war. I hope we can
stop the war. I wish that
there was no such
thing as war. I wish
that peace was all
over the world. My
heart sinks down

(2) When war is
Going on. I LOVE
PEACE!! I LOVE
PEACE!! I wish war
was love and peace is
what war should

be. When war's going
on, people get
killed and familys
get separated, and

I hate it. I want
this war to stop. I'm
sad because the war
is going on. I'm
sure that

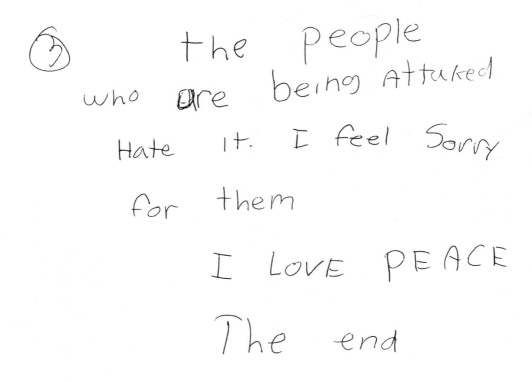

the people
who are being Attaked
Hate it. I feel Sorry
for them

I LOVE PEACE

The end

Sophia's prose piece, transcribed by her at age nine, was originally written when she was five. It shows what is possible for even a very young child to understand about the peacemaking process.

Julian

Peace

Large was the waterfall of peace
Until there became a block in the shape of a battle
And a large boulder rolled into the water
The rock meant pollution
Now the streams grow fewer
As the barriers grow larger
We must stop this water from draining away entirely
Or our world will be a planet
of total war.

Across a sea of blood
and a desert of human bones
There lies a land
of peace and life.
In that land There is the secret
Of existence and love
Now blood and bones
Rise up
Against this happy life.

References

Baer, J. (1994). "The Web We Weave: Creating the Fabric of Peacemaking." *Primary Voices K–6*, Vol.2, Number 4, Pages 12–16.

Best, R. (1989). *We've All Got Scars*. Indiana University Press.

Buchowski-Monin, M., Canadian Representative of *Children's Creative Response to Conflict*. Box 7068, Station J., Ottawa, Ontario, Canada, K2A 3Z6.

Burrell, C., Nyman, D., Azevedo, N., and Filmus, D. (1989). *The Peaceosaurus*. Toronto, Ontario, Canada: The DASosaurus Press. (Available from the Federation of Women Teachers' Associations of Ontario, 1260 Bay Street, Toronto, Ontario, Canada, M5R 2B8.)

Dillon, D. (1990) "Liberation Education: An Interview with Ira Shor." *Language Arts* 67:342–352.

Fine, E. (1987). "Marbles Lost, Marbles Found: Collaborative Production of Text." *Language Arts* 64:474–489.

Fine, E. (1989). "Collaborative Writing: Key to Unlocking the Silences of Children." *Language Arts* 66:501–509.

Fine, E. (1990). "Interrogating Silences: Collaborative Production of Dramatic Text in a Special Education Classroom." Unpublished thesis.

Fine, E. (1991). "Interrogating Silences, " in S. Stires (ed.) *With Promise: Redefining Reading and Writing for "Special Students*." New Hampshire: Heinemann.

Fine, E. (1994). "Peacemaking as a Tool for Change." *Primary Voices K–6*, Vol.2, Number 4, Pages 1–3.

Fine, E., Lacey, A., Baer, J. (1993). "Children as Peacemakers." *Democracy & Education*, Fall.

Fine, E., Lacey, A., Baer, J., and Rother, B. (December 1991/January 1992). "Children as Peacemakers." *FWTAO Newsletter*, Vol. 10, Number 3, Pages 2–10.

Grishina, N.G., (1934). *The Magic Squirrel*. New York: Lippincott.

Hart-Hewin, L. and Wells, J. (1988) *Borrow-a-Book*. Toronto: Scholastic.

King, R., and Squire, R. (1994). *Face to Face: Conflict Resolution in School, Bullying at School: Strategies for Prevention* (videos). King Squire Films Limited Distributor, 94 Borden Street, Toronto, Ontario, Canada M5S 2N1; telephone (416)922–6509.

Lacey, A. (1994). "Children Evolving into Peacemakers." *Primary Voices K–6*, Vol.2, Number 4, Pages 24–28.

Lacey, A. (1994). "Peacemaking as a Tool for Change." *Primary Voices K–6*, Vol.2, Number 4, Pages 24–28.

Li Preti, F. (1993). "Student Empowerment in a Conflict Resolution Program: An Evaluation." Unpublished thesis research project, York University, Toronto, Canada.

Li Preti, F. (1994). "Reflections." *Primary Voices K–6*, Vol.2, Number 4, Pages 12–16.

Paley, V. (1992). *You Can't Say You Can't Play*. Cambridge, MA: Harvard University Press.

Paxton-Beesley, R. (1991). *The Food Fight, Ta-Daa!* Toronto, Ontario, Canada: The DASosaurus Press. (Available from the Federation of Women Teachers' Associations of Ontario, 1260 Bay Street, Toronto, Ontario, Canada, M5R 2B8.)

Sadalla, G., Holmberg, M., and Halligan, J. (1990). *Conflict Resolution: An Elementary School Curriculum*. San Francisco, CA: The Community Board Program, Inc., 149 Ninth Street, San Francisco, California 94103 U.S.A.

Toronto Board of Education. (1989). *Math & Science Investigations*.

Annotated Bibliography

Canfield.J. and H.C. Wells. 1976. *100 Ways to Enhance Self-Concept in the Classroom*. Englewood Cliffs, NJ: Prentice-Hall.

   Activities to help build an affirming, positive, loving community in the classroom. Most appropriate for junior/intermediate.

Carlsson-Paige, N. and D. E. Levin. 1985. *Peace, War, and the Nuclear Threat*. Washington, DC: National Association for the Education of Young Children.

   How to help children cope with growing up in the nuclear age.

Clarke, J. and Dawson. 1989. *Growing Up Again*. New York: Harper Collins.

   For parents and teachers. Creative guidelines for establishing discipline and structure, setting limits, and showing love.

Drew, N. 1987. *Learning the Skills of Peacemaking*. Rolling Hills Estates, CA: Jalmar Press.

   Beginning with becoming peacemakers ourselves, then exploring our interconnectedness on a classroom, community, and global level.

Fine, E. and N. Norquay, editors. November 1994. *Primary Voices K–6* (journal). Urbana, IL: National Council of Teachers of English.

   Entire issue on conflict resolution and racism/equity.

Fugitt, E. 1983. *"He Hit Me Back First!"* Rolling Hills Estates, CA: Jalmar Press.

Techniques for fostering awareness of choice. Helping children develop self-acceptance, inner discipline, and the use of will.

Gibbs, J. 1987. *Tribes*. Santa Rosa, CA: Center Source Publications.
Building community in the classroom and encouraging responsible behavior through positive small group process. Focus on elementary age group.

Johnson, D. W. and R. T. Johnson. 1991. *Teaching Children to Be Peacemakers*. Edina, MN: Interaction Book Company.
Step-by-step skill-building training for analyzing and handling conflicts. Very thorough. Combines theory and activities for classroom use.

King, R. and R. Squire. 1994. *Face to Face: Conflict Resolution in School, Bullying at School: Strategies for Prevention* (videos). King Squire Films Limited Distributor, 94 Borden Street, Toronto, Ontario, Canada, M5S 2N1; telephone (416) 922-6509.

Face to Face (40 min.) shows how conflict resolution strategies can be taught and implemented at both the elementary and secondary levels, within the curriculum, in student mediation programs, and in class management and discipline.

Bullying at School (40 min.) examines the nature of bullying and demonstrates a wide range of preventative strategies at the elementary level.

Kreidler, W. J. 1984. *Creative Conflict Resolution*. Glenview, IL: Scott, Foresman and Company.
More than 200 activities for keeping peace in the classroom. Kreidler himself is a teacher. Highest praise to this well-organized and easy-to-use guide. Activities to raise awareness about anger, communication, and tolerance. My own copy is dog-eared.

Paley, V. G. 1992. *You Can't Say You Can't Play*. Cambridge, MA: Harvard University Press.
A brilliant and insightful teacher probes the questions of exclusion with her kindergarten children. Can we stop ourselves from hurting others' feelings? Stories from the classroom skillfully woven together with a fairy tale written by Paley herself.

Pike, G. and D. Selby. 1988. *Global Teacher, Global Learner*. London: Hodder and Stoughton.
Theory and activities to help create an affirmative environment and a sense of responsible connectedness in the global classroom.

Prutzman, P. 1988. *The Friendly Classroom for a Small Planet*. Philadelphia, PA: New Society Publishers.

    Children's Creative Response to Conflict Program. A classic handbook on creative approaches to living and problem solving. Cooperating, communicating, and affirming ourselves and each other. Loving attention to creating a supportive environment.

Sadalla, G., M. Holmberg, and J. Halligan. 1990. *Conflict Resolution: An Elementary School Curriculum*. San Francisco, CA: Community Board Program.

    Complete program of activities to begin a Conflict Managers' Program.

Wichert, S. 1989. *Keeping the Peace*. Philadelphia, PA: New Society Publishers.

    Practicing cooperation and conflict resolution with preschoolers. Helping children to learn to speak clearly and listen to each other. Contains lots of anecdotes and poses many provocative questions.

Children's Books

The following are just a few examples of books to use as discussion starters or as introductions to activities.

Allen, L. 1991. *Why Me?* Well Versed Publications, 427 Bloor Street West, Suite 109, Toronto, Ontario, Canada, M5S 1X7. ISBN 1-895248-02-7.

  A little girl's day begins badly and just keeps getting worse until it ends in an angry exchange with her mother. Tears are followed by sleep, but when morning comes there is the warmth of sunshine and reconciliation. Illustrated by Sherry Guppy.

Burrell, C., Nyman, D., Azevedo, N., & Filmus, D. 1989. *The Peaceosaurus*. Toronto, Ontario, Canada: The DASosaurus Press. (Available from the Federation of Women Teachers' Associations of Ontario, 1260 Bay Street, Toronto, Ontario, Canada M5R 2B8.) ISBN 0-9694338-0-8.

  The same story pictured above (see Introduction) is available as a published book for children.

Jones, R. 1991. *Matthew and Tilly*. New York: Dutton. ISBN 0-525-44684-2.

  After a big fight, two best friends discover how much they miss each other. This is a story about friendship, loneliness and reconciliation, set in a multicultural urban center. Illustrated by Beth Peck.

Lokhat, A. 1994. *Molly, Sue and Someone New*. TSAR Publications,

P.O. Box 6996, Station A, Toronto, Ontario, Canada, M5W 1X7. ISBN 0-920661-43-2.

This new picture book, written and illustrated by an undergraduate student in the Faculty of Education at York University, tells a simple story about three girls who cross racial boundaries to become friends. Though the issue of race is not well developed in this text about exclusion, the illustrations indicate that race is an issue. A skillful teacher might generate discussion by asking children to explore unspoken messages and form questions about the story.

Osborne, M. 1993. *Mermaid Tales from Around the World.* New York: Scholastic. ISBN 0-590-44377-1.

This picture book contains a collection of illustrated stories of mermaids and mermen of many races and cultures. It uses the fantasy of mermaids as a vehicle to explore a world view that rejects global centrality of any single culture, offering all children an affirming, respectful journey to self and others. Illustrated by Troy Howell.

Paxton-Beesley, R. 1991. *The Food Fight, Ta-Daa!* Toronto, Ontario, Canada: The DASosaurus Press. (Available from the Federation of Women Teachers' Associations of Ontario, 1260 Bay Street, Toronto, Ontario, Canada, M5R 2B8.) ISBN 0-9694338-1-6.

Robin's original script for the photo story (see pages 32–35:) was illustrated by cartoonist Carlos Freire and published as a book for children.

Peaceosaurus Chorus. 1990. A cassette tape: *Let's Talk About Peace.* Toronto, Ontario, Canada: The DASosaurus Press. (Available from the Federation of Women Teachers' Associations of Ontario, 1260 Bay Street, Toronto, Ontario, Canada, M5R 2B8.)

Sadu, I. 1992. *Name Calling.* Well Versed Publications, 427 Bloor Street West, Suite 109, Toronto, Ontario, Canada, M5S 1X7. ISBN 1-895248-04-3.

With the help of a school principal, Cindy and Jennifer resolve a conflict, which stops just short of mob violence within a racially diverse group of school children. Illustrated by Rasheeda Haneef.

Scholes, K. 1989. *Peace Begins with You.* Boston: Little, Brown. ISBN 0-316-77436-7.

The book begins as a personal discussion of different people's needs and wants and then explores how this potential source of conflicts can be resolved positively. Discussion moves from personal to global questions, complemented by beautiful color illustrations of artist Robert Ingpen.

Scieszka, J. 1989. *The True Story of the Three Little Pigs*. New York: Viking Penguin. ISBN 0-670-82759-2

Another version of the familiar story—from the wolf's point of view. Illustrated by Lane Smith.

Seuss, Dr. 1954/1982. *The Sneetches and Other Stories*. New York: Random House.

These stories engage young readers and encourage discussion of exclusion, tolerance, and problem solving.

Young, E. 1989. *LonPoPo*. New York: Philomel Books. ISBN 0-399-21619-7.

An intriguing Red Riding Hood story from China. Useful for beginning discussion on the concept of "versions." Illustrated by the author.

Credits

Cover photograph. This photograph first appeared on the cover of the December 1991/January 1992 issue of *Federation of Women Teachers' Association of Ontario Newsletter* as the cover story "Children as Peacemakers" which won the Educational Press Association of America Distinguished Achievement Award for Excellence in Educational Journalism.

Back Cover. Excerpt from "Children as Peacemakers" by Michele Landsberg. Reprinted with permission from The Toronto Star Syndicate.

Excerpts from "Reflections" by Franca LiPreti. From *Primary Voices K–6* (vol. 2, no. 4, November, 1994). Copyright 1994 by the National Council of Teachers of English. Reprinted with permission.

Portions of this text originally appeared in the following articles:

"Children as Peacemakers" by Esther Sokolov Fine, Ann Lacey, Joan Baer, and Barbara Rother. From *FWTAO Newsletter* (vol. 10, no. 3, 1991/92 December/January). Reprinted by permission of the Federation of Women Teachers' Associations of Ontario.

"Children Evolving into Peacemakers" by Ann Lacey. From *Primary Voices K–6* (vol. 2, no. 4, November, 1994). Copyright 1994 by the National Council of Teachers of English. Reprinted with permission.

"Peacemaking as a Tool for Change" by Esther Sokolov Fine. From *Primary Voices K–6* (vol. 2, no. 4, November, 1994). Copyright 1994 by the National Council of Teachers of English. Reprinted with permission.

"A Message from the Editors" by Esther Sokolov Fine and Naomi Norquay. From *Primary Voices K–6* (vol. 2, no. 4, November, 1994). Copyright 1994 by the National Council of Teachers of English. Reprinted with permission.

"The Web We Weave: Creating the Fabric of Peacemaking" by Joan Baer. From *Primary Voices K–6* (vol. 2, no. 4, November, 1994). Copyright 1994 by the National Council of Teachers of English. Reprinted with permission.